T0625078

# BRIDGES TO FEAR

## A COLLECTION OF STRANGE BUT TRUE STORIES

## Mitsu Yamamoto

# NEWBURY HOUSE READER  Level 3

# NEWBURY HOUSE READERS

This series of books will contain Readers at six proficiency levels for students of English. The vocabularies assumed, at this time, are:

| | | | |
|---|---|---|---|
| Level 1 | 300 to 500 words | Level 4 | 1000 to 1500 words |
| Level 2 | 500 to 750 words | Level 5 | 1500 to 2000 words |
| Level 3 | 750 to 1000 words | Level 6 | 2000 or more words |

The guiding grammatical structures for each level are:

Level 1: simple present, simple past, simple future
Level 2: as above plus present progressive, past progressive, future tense with *going to*
Level 3: as above plus present perfect tense
Level 4: as above plus future tense with *going to* in the past
Level 5: as above plus past perfect, future progressive
Level 6: as above plus past perfect, future progressive

*Series and book design by Diana Esterly.*
*Illustrations and calligraphy by Andrea Hayes.*

NEWBURY HOUSE PUBLISHERS, Inc.

Language Science
Language Teaching
Language Learning

ROWLEY, MASSACHUSETTS 01969

Copyright © 1977 by Newbury House Publishers, Inc. All rights reserved. No part of this book may be reproduced or transmitted in any form or by any means, electronic or mechanical, including photocopying, recording, or by any information storage and retrieval system, without permission in writing from the Publisher.

First printing: December 1977
Printed in the U.S.A.                    5    4    3

# Contents

# 1

## *Visit to an Eskimo Village*

Five strong dogs pulled Joe Labelle's **sled** over the snow to Lake Angikuni. Joe often visited Eskimo friends in a **village** near the **lake.** Though snow was falling, Joe saw the village less than a quarter of a mile away. He pushed his hat back from his ears and listened. He was surprised when he did not hear the dogs in the village.

Joe pulled his hat over his ears. Then he called to his dogs to go faster. Soon he shouted "Hello!" There was no answer. He shouted louder. Still no answer. Joe stopped the sled and listened carefully. The only noise was the wind.

The dogs looked back at Joe and waited for his order. Joe's hands and feet were like ice, but he did not move yet. Thirty people lived in the village. But not one person answered him! His heart jumped.

Joe was a **trapper**, and in the Far North a trapper must be strong and brave. A trapper travels alone with his dogs in a country full of dangerous animals. Joe never was afraid of animals because he carried a **rifle** and a knife. But he was afraid of this quiet village. There was trouble in it. But Joe did not go away; he drove slowly forward with his rifle in his hand.

Joe left his dogs and sled near the first house. His friends always ran to him, but not today. Now he heard only the noise of his **own** feet on the ice and snow. He stopped at the door of the first house, but he did not knock. He held his rifle in both hands and pushed the door open with one foot. The place was empty.

Joe walked to the next house. Empty. And to the next. Empty. Soon he was running from house to house. All the houses were empty. "Where are the people?" he asked himself. Next he shouted, "Where are you? This is Joe Labelle!"

Then he had an idea. He ran to the middle of the village and called the names of his special friends. Then he said, "I know that you saw my sled and heard my dogs before I arrived. And I know that you are playing a game with me. But come out now, and we will laugh together." There was no answer.

Joe told himself that he must look into every house again. So he did. Slowly he looked at everything—clothes, pots, beds. Everything seemed ordinary. In the first house a child's coat was on the floor. Someone was fixing a hole in the pocket. There was a **needle** still in the material. In all the houses there was still food in pots over dead fires. Also the rifles of all the families were still in their houses. Joe did not understand this. In Alaska a man always takes his rifle with him when he goes out. Either he is looking for small animals for food, or he is afraid of large and dangerous animals. If they left their rifles behind, the people went out only for a few minutes. They left their work and their hot food, and hurried outside. Why? What happened then? Where did they go? Joe did not know the answers. But he did know that people traveled out of the village only by boat or by dogsled.

He left the houses and walked to Lake Angikuni. The wind

was stronger there. Soon Joe found the boats. They were broken by storms. One friend's boat was almost in pieces.

Then Joe said to himself, "The boats are still here because they were not important. The people left in their sleds." For the first time since he arrived, Joe felt happy. He ran to the four trees behind the houses; that was the dogs' place in the village. "The dogs will not be there," he told himself. "The people went in their sleds, and the dogs went with them." But when he arrived at the trees, Joe's eyes became round with surprise. The place by the trees was not empty. The dogs were there—dead! They looked small, like cats, because their bodies were so thin.

Joe began to feel sick. The boats and the sled dogs were still in the village, so the people must be here, too. But Joe knew that he was alone. A heavier snow was falling now. It covered his hat. But his head felt hot.

"Get the **Mounties**," Joe ordered himself. "They will explain it all." He felt a little better when he thought about the Mounties. Their job is helping people in trouble, and they do it well.

Joe left the dead animals and started back to his own dogs and sled. Then he found the strangest surprise in the village—two **piles** of stones beside a long hole. Suddenly his feet felt heavy. His mouth was dry. He knew that he must look at the stones and the hole more carefully, but he did not want to. He walked through the snow very slowly.

He stopped beside the hole and saw that it was empty. It was an Eskimo **grave**, but there was no body in it. Joe knew that Eskimoes never open a grave again. Why was this grave different? Where was the body? Joe turned and ran from the grave. Quicker than a cat, he jumped on his sled and drove out of the village.

After a trip of three days, Joe arrived at the offices of the Mounties and started to tell his story. The Mounties' first question was, "Labelle, do you drink much?" Other questions followed. Joe answered their questions, and the

Mounties believed him. They sent ten men to the village. Joe went with them, because he wanted answers too.

The Mounties looked at everything in the village for months. They did not learn any new facts, and it was not possible to explain the old facts. This happened in 1930, and there are still no answers. The people of the village were not found—dead or alive. The empty grave was not explained. Joe Labelle thinks that he had a bad dream and that it became real.

### New Words

**a grave**   The place where a dead body is put; usually a hole in the ground.

**a lake**   Much water; not the sea.

**the Mounties**   A short name for the Royal Canadian Mounted Police, the Canadian policemen who ride horses.

**a needle**   Something we use when we make clothes.

**own**   His (or hers, mine, yours, its . . . )

**a pile**   Many things close together, some on top of others.

**a rifle**   Something to kill with.

**a sled**   Something in which to ride on top of snow.

**a trapper**   Someone who catches animals.

**a village**   A place where a few people live. A village has more than one house, but a village is smaller than a town.

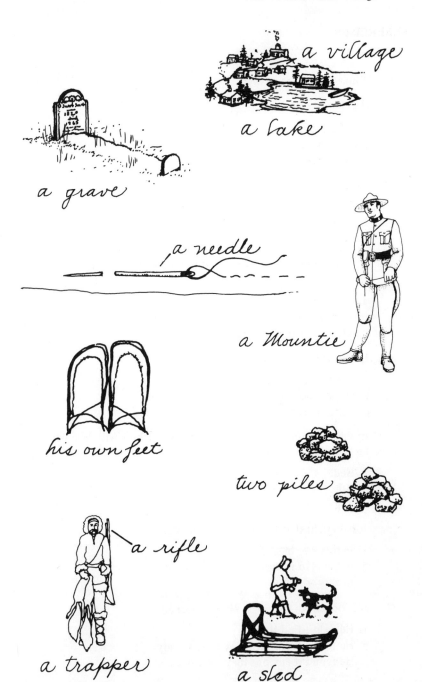

a village

a lake

a grave

a needle

a Mountie

his own feet

two piles

a rifle

a trapper

a sled

## EXERCISES

A.   Choose the right answer.

1.   Joe Labelle was

    a. an Eskimo.
    b. a trapper.
    c. a Mountie.

2.   How many people lived in the village?

    a. Thirty.
    b. Forty-five.
    c. Sixty.

3.   Soon after he arrived, Joe called to his friends. He thought that they were

    a. fixing dinner.
    b. in their houses.
    c. playing a game with him.

4.   In all the houses, Joe found

    a. children's coats on the ground.
    b. food in pots over dead fires.
    c. dangerous animals.

5.   In the Far North, a man always takes something with him when he goes out. It is his

    a. sled.
    b. rifle.
    c. dog.

6.   Joe thought that the people left the village

    a. in boats or in sleds.
    b. in boats or in cars.
    c. in cars or in sleds.

7.   Joe looked for the dogs. What happened?

    a. He didn't find them.
    b. He found them, and they were hungry.
    c. He found them, but they were dead.

8.  Joe saw a hole. It was

    a. a pile of stones.
    b. an empty grave.
    c. the dogs' place in the village.

9.  At first, the Mounties thought that Joe

    a. drank too much.
    b. was stupid.
    c. had a strange dream.

10.  When the Mounties went to the village,

    a. they found the people—dead.
    b. they found the people—alive.
    c. they didn't find the people.

B.  Choose the answer which explains the word (*like this*) that looks different.

1.  It was an Eskimo *grave.*

    a. A bed for an animal.
    b. A place to put a boat.
    c. A hole for a dead body.

2.  There was a *needle* still in the material.

    a. Something we use when we make clothes.
    b. Something to kill dangerous animals.
    c. Something to cook food.

3.  He saw two *piles* of stones.

    a. Some stones, one in front of another.
    b. Some stones, one on top of another.
    c. A pot full of stones.

4.  Joe was a white *trapper.*

    a. He caught animals.
    b. He visited Eskimo villages.
    c. He was a Mountie.

5.  Joe saw the *village* less than a quarter of a mile away.

    a. A place where many people live.
    b. A place where nobody lives.
    c. A place where a few people live.

C.    Put the right word in every **sentence**.

**sentence**    A number
of words which are
used to tell one's
thoughts.

over, like, afraid, either, beside, empty, still, alive, with, outside

1.    They went _____ in boats or in sleds.
2.    This happened in 1930 and there are _____ no answers.
3.    His hands and feet were _____ ice.
4.    He stopped _____ the hole.
5.    The people were not found–dead or _____ .
6.    The dogs pulled the sled _____ the snow.
7. .  He is not _____ of large and dangerous animals.
8.    You are playing a game _____ me.
9.    They left their houses and went _____ .
10.   The grave was _____ .

D.    Make sentences with these words. Keep the words in the same order.

1.    shout, hello, friend
2.    trapper, strong, brave
3.    Joe, walk, house
4.    run, middle, village
5.    you, play, game, me
6.    Joe, find, boat
7.    people, go, sled
8.    see, pile, stone
9.    hole, empty
10.   Joe, tell, story

E.    Write T (for True) if you think that the sentence is true. Write F (for **False**) if you think that it is not true.

**false**    Not true.

1.    Joe was a trapper.
2.    Ten people lived in the village.
3.    Joe's friends ran to meet him.
4.    Trappers travel alone.

5.  Joe thought that his friends were playing a game.
6.  All the families took their rifles with them.
7.  Joe found the boats.
8.  The boats were broken.
9.  Joe didn't find the dogs.
10. The Mounties knew where the people were.

# 2

## The Luck of James Bartley

My name is James Bartley. I am twenty-two years old, and I fix shoes here in Gloucester, England. Also, I am famous. People—important people and ordinary people—arrive in this town every day just to see me and to talk to me. Do you wonder how this is possible? The reason is that I am the James Bartley who was on the ship *Star of the East.*

It was my first time at sea. We killed **whales,** and the work was hard and dirty. But I was strong, and I thought that it was exciting. Also it was my first trip away from home. In those days I wanted to see the world. Now, just one year later, I will not ride to the next town. My customers find me in my store every day. I travel only between my store and my home.

So, because I was young, I enjoyed myself. I liked the sun over the water and the storms with their black clouds. I liked my new friends and our dangerous work. This happy time ended for me on March 3, 1891, at ten o'clock in the morning. That date will be put on the stone over my head when I am dead and in my grave.

That morning we saw a crowd of whales. The **captain** told us to put the small boats into the water. We jumped into them and pushed away from the *Star of the East.* Then we followed one whale who was as tall as a bridge and as long as two fields. She was black, and the water shone on her body.

When we threw our **harpoon** at her, it went straight into her heart. The whale almost jumped out of the water. She threw her body against our little boat. The boat broke like a match, and we all fell into the sea.

The water was *very* cold. Those of us in the water were shouting at the men in the other boats. A few were helped from the sea. Others were dying. My hand touched a piece of wood from my boat, but the sea pulled it away from me. I was tired and afraid. Then a great wall of water fell on me. It moved like a fast river and carried me with it. I saw an eye—the ugly, thin eye of a whale! It is in my dreams to this day.

I called for my mother, the captain, my friends! Now I was not in the sea; I was in a wet, red room. The room moved like the sea, up and down. There were many thin white stones. When I fell against them, they cut me like knives.

Another river of water filled the red room and carried me to a big hole. I fell down into the hole like a leaf in a storm. My arm was hurt when the water threw me against something heavy. The thing was as tall as myself. It was like red meat, with a white tree inside. The tree seemed to be alive; it was moving slowly forward and back, forward and back. There was a great fork in the middle of the tree. Then I saw that it was not a fork; it was the harpoon from the *Star of the East.* I was standing in front of a whale's heart! I was inside a whale's body!

I shut my eyes quickly. "This is only a bad dream," I told myself. "I will wake soon in my bed in Gloucester, or back on the *Star.* I do not really see a heart." But I heard a noise like a heart. The thing was opening and shutting like my own heart. I covered my ears with my hands, but still I heard it. Suddenly I was sick. Later I washed my mouth with water. I did not cry or shout or hope. I knew that I was sitting beside a whale's heart, that the whale was alive, and that I was inside the whale. I was afraid to die and afraid to live.

It was very hot, and my head hurt. My wet clothes were heavy, and my arm was now black and blue. I slept, and woke, and slept again. At one time my grandmother, who died last year, was standing beside me. "Jamie," she said, "here is some cheese for your lunch." She put the cheese in my hand, but it changed to something large and wet. Then I woke and saw that I was holding part of a dead fish. I was still inside the whale.

I counted one, two, three hours—or perhaps it was only minutes. I was hotter and sicker. Soon I did not wake up between my ugly dreams.

Three weeks later I woke in bed on the *Star of the East.* I was alive and safe. The captain told me the story. They caught the whale at two o'clock in the afternoon that day—March 3. While they were carefully cutting the fat off the whale, one man saw a dark cloud inside the whale. The cloud was as large as a person. This was not usual, so they began to cut as fast as possible. When they found me, I was almost dead.

So I am famous now. People look at me; newspapers say that all my thoughts are interesting news; and I am the most popular man in Gloucester. But I feel lonely. I am the only person in the world who was food for a whale—and is still alive.

**New Words**

**a captain**   The most important man on a ship.

**a harpoon**   Something to kill whales.

**a whale**   A very large sea animal.

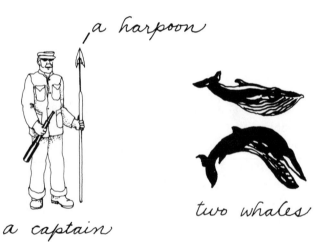

*a harpoon*

*a captain*

*two whales*

**EXERCISES**

A.   Choose the right answer.

1.   James Bartley is famous because he
     a. fixes shoes.
     b. was eaten by a whale.
     c. helped to catch a whale.

2.   James Bartley's ship was
     a. *Star of the East.*
     b. *Star of the West.*
     c. *North Star.*

3.   Did he like his job on the ship?
     a. No.
     b. Yes.
     c. He doesn't say.

4.   When the men saw the whales, they
     a. were afraid.
     b. got into small boats and followed one whale.
     c. followed the whales in their ship.

5.   The men hurt the whale with a
     a. knife.
     b. rifle.
     c. harpoon.

6.   When James Bartley was in "a wet, red room," he was in
     a. a room on the ship.
     b. a room in his dream.
     c. the whale's mouth.

7.   What was "like red meat, with a large tree inside"?
     a. A piece of cheese.
     b. The eye of the whale.
     c. The whale's heart.

8.   When he was inside the whale, James Bartley was
     a. hot
     b. cold.
     c. He doesn't say.

9.   He dreamed about

   a. the captain of his ship.
   b. his mother.
   c. his grandmother.

10.   When the men found James Bartley, he was

   a. almost dead.
   b. asleep.
   c. dead.

B.   Choose the answer which explains the word or words that look different.

1.   I am *famous.*

   a. Pretty.
   b. Safe.
   c. A lot of people know me.

2.   My *customers* find me in my store.

   a. People who want me to fix their shoes.
   b. People who want me to tell them my story.
   c. People who want me to buy something.

3.   Our work was *dangerous.*

   a. It was not interesting.
   b. It was not easy.
   c. It was not safe.

4.   *It is in my dreams to this day.*

   a. I still dream about it.
   b. I am still there today.
   c. I do not think about it.

5.   *The thing was as tall as myself.*

   a. It was taller than me.
   b. I was taller than it.
   c. We were the same size.

C.   Put the right word in every sentence.

   at, away, between, against, like, forward, inside, to, again, last

1.   She threw her body _____ our little boat.
2.   It was my first trip _____ from home.

3. It was moving slowly, _____ and back.
4. I was afraid _____ live.
5. My grandmother died _____ year.
6. I slept and woke and slept _____ .
7. It was my first time _____ sea.
8. I was _____ a whale's body.
9. It broke _____ a match.
10. I travel only _____ my store and my home.

D. Make sentences with these words. Keep the words in the same order.

1. people, arrive, town
2. work, hard, dirty
3. want, see, world
4. follow, black, whale
5. like, leaf, storm
6. hear, noise, heart
7. cover, ear, hand
8. put, cheese, hand
9. captain, tell, story
10. cloud, large, person

E. Write T (for True) if you think that the sentence is true. Write F (for False) if you think that it is not true.

1. James Bartley lives in England.
2. The whale was blue.
3. The harpoon hit the whale.
4. The whale broke the boat.
5. James Bartley saw the whale's eye.
6. There was a knife in the whale's heart.
7. His grandmother gave him some cheese in his dream.
8. He counted six hours.
9. He woke up a week later.
10. James Bartley is happy now.

# 3

## The Man Who Dreamed the News

Newspaper offices are very busy places. Usually they are noisy with people and telephones. But when the day's paper is written, and is for sale on the streets, everything becomes quiet for a few hours. Newspapers like *The Boston Globe* keep only one man in the office then.

Edward Samson wrote for the *Globe.* On the night of August 28, 1883, he was the man alone in the office. His only job that night was to answer the telephone. But the telephone stayed quiet, and soon Samson was asleep. After twenty minutes he woke because someone was shouting, "It's Pralape, near Java!"

He smiled when he saw that he was shouting himself. But then he remembered his dream. It seemed as real as the table beside him. He tried to put a match to a cigarette, but his hand jumped too much. The dream was still in his head.

Samson chose a pencil and began to write. "There is an **island** near Java. Its name is Pralape. A **volcano** on the island just

21

**erupted.** It sent fire and stones down on the island like rain from the sky. It killed people, animals, and chickens. It broke boats, bridges, and houses.

"A mother and her children ran to the sea, but a river of fire from the volcano caught them. A man climbed a tree to be safe, but both the man and the tree were burned. At one place there was a large garden; it was green with plants of many kinds. In a minute it was changed to hot, black ground."

Samson wrote for half an hour. His story ended when the volcano erupted for the second time. It broke the island into pieces, and the pieces fell into the sea. The people were gone; the houses and trees were gone; the island itself was gone. There was only the sea—and the sea was angry. When the island fell into the sea, the sea moved. There were walls of water as high as hills. Pralape Island was dead.

Before he put down his pencil, Samson wrote the word "Important" on the first page of his story. He did this because it was an important dream. He usually forgot his dreams at once. Then he turned off the lights in the office, and went home.

Later that morning, another **writer** saw the story with "Important" on it. He put it in the box of news for the newspaper. That night all Boston read about the volcano on Pralape. The *Globe* was the only newspaper with the story, and it was glad of its luck.

Then newspapers in other towns used the story from the *Globe*. And they sent their writers out for more news on Pralape. The writers asked the *Globe*. But there they found red faces. Nobody knew of anything about Pralape Island. There was no news from Java. Ed Samson lost his job. The *Globe* explained that the story on Pralape was an honest mistake. They said that it was not a trick to sell more newspapers than usual.

A few days later, Ed Samson was asking for work at another newspaper in Boston. While he was in the office, a writer arrived with some news. All over the world the sea was moving. There were great walls of water as high as hills. Nobody knew the reason for this, but it was not because of storms.

Then ships arrived with news of a volcano on an island near Java. The men on these ships told the story of Ed Samson's dream. The same volcano erupted; the same people died; the same island was no more. But there was one thing different. The name of the island was Krakatoa, not Pralape.

At once the *Globe* gave Samson back his job. He wrote all the stories about Krakatoa. His photograph was put on the front page of the newspaper beside his stories. He became famous. He was the man who dreamed the news. People at the *Globe* were happy again, and people from other newspapers no longer laughed at them.

A few years later someone found a fact in an old book and sent Ed Samson a letter about it. The book showed different parts of the world and told their names. People used these names over a hundred years before, but later some of the names were forgotten. One island near Java was called Pralape in the old book. But by 1883 it was known as Krakatoa.

## New Words

**to erupt**   To break out suddenly; suddenly to send out something that was closed in.

**an island**   Earth in the middle of water.

**a volcano**

**a writer**   Someone who writes.

to erupt

an island

a volcano

a writer

## EXERCISES

A.   Choose the right answer.

1.   Edward Samson worked

   a. for a newspaper in Java.
   b. at night for a Boston newspaper.
   c. all day for a Boston newspaper.

2.   On August 28, 1883, he

   a. was very busy in the office.
   b. slept through the night.
   c. slept a short time.

3.   How many times did the volcano erupt?

   a. Once.
   b. Twice.
   c. Three times.

4.   After he wrote the story, Samson

   a. ate a sandwich.
   b. went to sleep.
   c. went home.

5.   Why was Samson's story in the *Globe*?

   a. Because another writer found it and thought that it was an important news story.
   b. Because Samson put it in the box of news for the newspaper.
   c. Because it was an interesting story.

6.   What happened when there was no news from Java?

   a. The *Globe* tried to sell more newspapers than usual.
   b. Ed Samson lost his job.
   c. Other writers asked the *Globe* for news.

7.   Samson's dream was true, but there was one thing different—the name of the

   a. volcano.
   b. island.
   c. ship.

8.   When they knew that his story was true, the *Globe*

   a. gave Samson back his job.

       b. sent Samson to Java.

       c. sent Samson an old book.

9.   Samson was famous because he

       a. worked for a newspaper.

       b. got his job back.

       c. dreamed the news.

10.   The island in Samson's dream was once called

       a. Pralape, but was later called Krakatoa.

       b. Java, but was later called Pralape.

       c. Krakatoa, but was later called Pralape.

B.   Choose the answer which explains the word or words that look different.

1.   It was an *honest* mistake.

       a. Stupid.

       b. Important.

       c. Real.

2.   Ed Samson *lost his job.*

       a. He went to work for another newspaper.

       b. The *Globe* said, "You cannot work for us any longer."

       c. He did not want to work for the *Globe* any longer.

3.   His photograph was put on the *front page.*

       a. Page 1.

       b. Page 2.

       c. Page 3.

4.   By 1883 *it was known as* Krakatoa.

       a. Its name was Krakatoa.

       b. Nobody knew its name.

       c. A few people called it Krakatoa.

5.   *He usually forgot his dreams.*

       a. He always remembered his dreams.

       b. He sometimes remembered his dreams.

       c. He never remembered his dreams.

C.   Put the right word in every sentence.

       who, for, as, near, into, about, back, through, many, than

1.   The pieces fell _____ the sea.

2.   The *Globe* gave Samson _____ his job.

3.   It seemed _____ real as the table.

4.   It was green with plants of _____ kinds.

5.   All Boston read _____ the volcano.

6.   The man _____ dreamed the news was Ed Samson.

7.   There is an island _____ Java.

8.   His job was to stay in the office _____ the night.

9.   It was not a trick to sell more newspapers _____ usual.

10.  He worked _____ a Boston newspaper.

D.   Make sentences with these words. Keep the words in the same order.

1.   put, match, cigarette

2.   volcano, island, erupt

3.   mother, run, sea

4.   man, tree, burn

5.   turn, light, office

6.   Boston, read, volcano

7.   Ed, lose, job

8.   Ed, ask, work

9.   ship, arrive, news

10.  write, story, Krakatoa

E.   Write T (for True) if you think that the sentence is true. Write F (for False) if you think that it is not true.

1.   Ed Samson worked for the Boston *Globe*.

2.   His job was to answer the telephone.

3.   Ed smiled when he remembered his dream.

4.   It was raining in his dream.

5.   Ed usually forgot his dreams.

6.   He turned on the lights in the office, and went home.

7.   Nobody believed the story in the *Globe*.

8.   The *Globe* just wanted to sell more newspapers than usual.

9.   Ed lost his job, and then he got it back.

10.  Krakatoa was once called Pralape.

# 4

## A Fine Afternoon in December

Once I watched airplanes in the sky over my yard. I liked them because they were so beautiful and fast, and because my husband flew an Avenger. Now I cry when I see an airplane. I think of these lonely years without John. How did he die? I do not know. And that is the worst thing.

I remember everything about that last day. The date was December 5, 1945. The weather was fine. I was glad, because John was flying that afternoon. It was just the usual trip; five Avengers followed the same orders every few days. We wives knew the number of miles and hours, so we always cooked dinner a little later on those nights. The Avengers flew east over the sea for 160 miles, turned north for 40 miles, and then came home. It was not much of a trip, and it was always over the same part of the sea. Why was it different that December afternoon?

John was living his last few hours, but we did not know it. We ate an early lunch. John did not like a heavy meal before he flew. So lunch was just sandwiches, milk, and my special cake. I never make it now. Then John said goodbye, kissed me, and drove away.

This was my afternoon: I washed our glasses and plates and did the shopping. It was very cold but beautiful outside. At the store I bought a chicken, cheese, oranges, and cigarettes for John. I wrote a letter to my sister. A little after four o'clock, I cleaned the chicken and thought about dinner with John.

This was John's afternoon: He arrived at FNS (Florida Naval Station) at fifteen minutes after one. He changed his clothes, then listened to the engine of his Avenger. At quarter to two, he and the other men received the usual orders from FNS and put their watches to the same time. At two o'clock, John's radio told him the weather and ordered him into the sky. He flew off, and the other Avengers followed. They traveled east, turned north, and then turned for the second time. They were coming home. It was quarter to four.

FNS was ready with orders for the Avengers, because there was a chance of snow over the airport. But John's voice came over the radio:

*JOHN*: "Hello, FNS, hello, FNS. Where are we?"

*FNS*: "Hello, Avenger One. Ask the other airplanes. We do not know."

*JOHN*: "I've asked the other Avengers already. They're not certain, either. Help us."

*FNS*: "Are you still over the sea?"

*JOHN*: "Yes."

*FNS*: "How many miles from FNS?"

*JOHN*: "About 225. We have plenty of gas. But we are lost. Please answer, FNS. Where are we?"

*FNS*: "Sorry, Avenger One. We still don't know."

*JOHN*: "Does this help? We can see a . . . "

*FNS*: "Don't stop. We are listening. Avenger One, call us, call us. Avenger One! Avenger One!"

The radio on Avenger One was dead.

FNS sent out a boat at once. Then they called me on the telephone. I hurried to the Station. I told myself that John is always lucky. But in my heart I was afraid to hope.

By now it was dark. But the boat that was looking for the Avengers was very large, with many lights. We waited and waited. The boat's radio did not answer FNS. The boat was gone—just like the Avengers!

Now I cried. But FNS acted. Their telephones and radios were busy. Twenty boats were sent out, and more than 250 airplanes. They looked everywhere. Of course they hoped to find the Avengers and the first boat. But they also looked for men who were hurt, engines or pieces of the airplanes, gas on the sea, clothing—anything. They found nothing and nobody.

How did John die? Where? Why? I cannot be happy again because I am still guessing.

**EXERCISES**

A.   Choose the right answer.

1.   On December 5, 1945

    a. it was raining.
    b. the weather was fine.
    c. The writer does not tell us about the weather.

2.   John flew with _____ other Avengers.

    a. three
    b. four
    c. five

3.   In the afternoon, John's wife

    a. visited her sister.
    b. ate chicken, cheese, and oranges.
    c. went to the store, then wrote a letter.

4.   John was at FNS for

    a. 45 minutes.
    b. half an hour.
    c. an hour.

5.   The Avengers flew

    a. east and then north.
    b. north and then east.
    c. south and then east.

6.   When John spoke on the radio, he asked,

    a. "Where are you?"
    b. "Where are the other airplanes?"
    c. "Where are we?"

7.   When John spoke on the radio, he was over the

    a. sea, about 225 miles from FNS.
    b. sea, about 150 miles from FNS.
    c. ground, about 250 miles from FNS.

8.   What happened to the first boat that FNS sent out to look for the Avengers?

    a. It was dark.
    b. Nobody knows.
    c. It had no gas.

9. FNS sent out

    a. twenty boats and more than 250 airplanes.
    b. twenty boats and more than 100 airplanes.
    c. fifteen boats and more than 250 airplanes.

10. What did they find?

    a. Gas on the sea.
    b. Pieces of the airplanes.
    c. Nothing.

B. Choose the answer which explains the word or words that look different.

1. It was just the *usual* trip.

    a. Nothing was different.
    b. Everything was different.
    c. It was a special day.

2. Five Avengers *followed* the same *orders.*

    a. They flew behind another airplane.
    b. They flew one behind the other.
    c. They did as they were told.

3. *John did not like a heavy meal.*

    a. He did not want a lot to eat.
    b. He did not want a small meal.
    c. He wanted a large meal.

4. John *drove away.*

    a. He left on a bicycle.
    b. He left in a car.
    c. He arrived in a car.

5. *There was a chance of snow.*

    a. Snow was certain.
    b. It was snowing.
    c. Snow was possible.

C. Put the right word in every sentence.

because, just, into, off, second, over, already, either, plenty, everywhere

1. His radio ordered him _____ the sky.
2. John's voice came _____ the radio.

3.    I don't know, and he doesn't know _____ .

4.    They looked _____ , but they found nothing.

5.    I liked them _____ they were so beautiful and fast.

6.    He flew _____ .

7.    I've asked them _____ ; shall I ask them again?

8.    We have _____ of gas.

9.    It was _____ the usual trip.

10.   They turned once, and then they turned a _____ time.

D.    Make sentences with these words. Keep the words in the same order.

1.    watch, airplane, sky

2.    eat, early, lunch

3.    store, buy, chicken

4.    write, letter, sister

5.    I, busy, kitchen

6.    listen, engine, airplane

7.    John, radio, dead

8.    boat, large, lights

9.    airplanes, boats, send out

10.   hope, find, Avengers

E.    Write T (for True) if you think that the sentence is true. Write F (for False) if you think that it is not true.

1.    The writer's husband is dead.

2.    She knows how he died.

3.    She remembers nothing about his last day.

4.    He died in the winter.

5.    She cooked dinner later when he was flying.

6.    The Avengers usually flew about 400 miles.

7.    John's last meal was breakfast.

8.    The writer never makes her special cake now.

9.    She bought bread at the store.

10.   She wrote to her sister.

# 5

## The Coffins of Barbados

I have always lived and worked in Barbados. I did not choose my job. It was my father's job, too, and my grandfather's. Our family builds **crypts.** A crypt is a small or large house of stones, half underground, for the **coffins** of dead people. There are many crypts here in Barbados. Some were built by my grandfather about 1840, and some are older.

Part of my job is to open old crypts, too. If the family already has a crypt, the crypt is opened when somebody in the family dies. Eight very strong men work for me. It takes eight men to move a dead body in its heavy coffin. We carry the coffin into the crypt, and the family tells us the right place to put it down. Then we close the crypt. I myself shut the door, lock it, and give the key to the family.

But now all eight of my men are afraid to go into any crypt on Barbados. They will still build a new crypt, but they will not open an old one.

The trouble began when we opened the crypt of a famous man. I will not use his name, because his family is angry with me—and with my dead grandfather. I will call him Body Three. In the 1840s, Body Three was not yet famous, and he was poor. When he died, my grandfather put him into a crypt. This crypt was owned by another family, and there were two other coffins in it—Body One and Body Two. Nobody opened the crypt after Body Three was put in. The door was locked, and stones were put against it, too. Then Body Three became famous, and his family decided to move his coffin. They paid for a very large and expensive new crypt, which my men and I built.

When the new crypt was ready, my men and I went to the old crypt for the coffin. I knew that the door was covered by plants and a small tree. So my men carried knives and axes. After two hours' work, the door was clean. Then we carried away the stones in front of it. That was another hour's work. Of course the door was still locked. I tried the key, but it did not turn. So we made a hole in the door. When the hole was large enough, I put my arm through it to open the door from the inside. I pushed against the door, but it did not move. So two men pushed with me. Still the door did not move. Next, all nine of us pushed together. This time the door moved a little. We rested, then pushed again. The door moved slowly, a little, then more, more . . .

Then there was a loud noise inside the crypt! Now the door opened easily, and I walked into the crypt. My men say that, just then, a cloud covered the sun. I looked for the reason for the loud noise. And I found it: the coffin of Body One was on the floor. It was broken because it fell from the wall to the floor.

It was dark inside the crypt. So I waited for the sun to shine again. When it did, I saw that Body Two's coffin was on the floor, too. Then I looked for the important coffin—Body Three's. It was not in the crypt!

I shouted to my men, "Bring me a light!" When they did, I walked slowly along the walls of the crypt. I felt the cold stones of the walls. Was there another door? No, there was not. There were only two coffins, and they were both on the floor. Who moved them? And who took Body Three away? These were questions without answers.

\* \* \* \* \* \*

Then I received an order to open a large crypt. My men were still afraid, but they needed the money. Also, they knew this crypt. A large family owned it, and it was often necessary for us to open it. Now the grandmother was dead. When I turned the key in the door, my men stood back. I held a light over my head and went in alone.

It was hard to believe my eyes. There were twenty coffins all over the floor. Some were on top of others. Not one was in its right place. They were thrown about like boats in a storm. My heart began to jump, and my mouth dropped open stupidly. I tried to call my men, but my voice was only as loud as a chicken's. I turned and ran from the crypt.

We went to the telephone and called the police and the family who owned the crypt. A few brave people from the town arrived with them. Soon there were about fifty people inside and outside the crypt. They talked and talked, but did not explain a thing. My men and I stayed far away from the crypt. We were all afraid. But the family gave us a lot of money; so we put the coffins back in their right places. The police promised to watch the crypt through the night.

By the next morning, all Barbados knew the news. The police tried to keep visitors back. But my men and I were glad that there was a crowd. It seemed less dangerous with so many people there. At noon the sad family arrived with the coffin of their dead grandmother. Many of them cried when my men carried the old woman's coffin to the crypt. Then the crowd was quiet while the police opened the door to the crypt. I told my men to go inside. They walked slowly forward. Then they stopped. Then they dropped the coffin and ran!

I ran away too. But first I looked quickly into the crypt. The coffins were all over the floor again. Again, some were on top of others. A few were broken.

Now people believe that some dead bodies are angry. They think that these dead people are ordering us not to touch certain crypts. But which crypts? We do not know. So my men and I do not work any more. People mostly stay in their houses; they never walk near the crypts. We all understand this dangerous fact: in Barbados dead bodies are not dead. They live among us.

## New Words

**a coffin**   A box for the body of a dead person.

*coffins*

**a crypt**   A stone house for the coffins of dead people.

*a crypt*

**EXERCISES**

A.   Choose the right answer.

1.   The man called Body Three died

    a. but we do not know when.
    b. last year.
    c. in the 1840s.

2.   How many men work for the writer?

    a. Eight.
    b. Nine.
    c. Twelve.

3.   The writer and his men went to open Body Three's crypt. They took knives and axes because

    a. they were afraid.
    b. the door was covered by plants and a small tree.
    c. Body Three was famous.

4.   What happened when the writer walked into the crypt?

    a. A cloud covered the sun.
    b. There was a loud noise.
    c. The men ran away.

5.   What did he find in the crypt?

    a. Body Three's coffin was on the floor.
    b. Nothing—the crypt was empty.
    c. Two coffins were on the floor, and Body Three's coffin was not in the crypt.

6.   The writer and his men opened another crypt. The men were afraid but they did the job because

    a. their grandmother was dead.
    b. they needed the money, and they knew that crypt.
    c. a large family owned it.

7.   What did the writer find in this second crypt?

    a. Twenty boats.
    b. Twenty chickens.
    c. Twenty coffins all over the floor.

8.   The family gave the men a lot of money, so they

    a. put the coffins back in their right places.

    b. watched the crypt through the night.

    c. called the police.

9. At noon the next day

    a. the men put the coffins back in their right places.

    b. the police arrived.

    c. the family arrived with their grandmother's coffin.

10. People believe that

    a. some dead bodies are angry.

    b. the police moved the coffins.

    c. people stay in their houses.

B. Choose the answer which explains the word or words which look different.

1. We went to the old crypt for the *coffin.*

    a. Key.

    b. Dead body.

    c. Wooden box for a dead body.

2. It was very *large and expensive.*

    a. It was big and it cost a lot of money.

    b. It was big and it cost a little money.

    c. It was small and it cost a lot of money.

3. *After two hours' work, the door was clean.*

    a. The men must work for two hours to clean the door.

    b. The men worked for two hours, and then the door was clean.

    c. If the men work for two hours, the door will be clean.

4. When the hole was large enough, I put my arm through *it.*

    a. The door.

    b. The hole.

5. *Just then,* a cloud covered the sun.

    a. A cloud covered the sun at the same time that I walked into the crypt.

    b. A cloud covered the sun just a few minutes before I walked in.

    c. After I walked in, then a cloud covered the sun.

C. Put the right word in every sentence.

always, right, yet, against, ready, by, away, enough, together, without

1. In the 1840s, Body Three was not _____ famous.
2. When the hole was large _____, I put my arm through it.
3. The door was locked, and stones were put _____ it.
4. When it was _____, we went to the old crypt for the coffin.
5. Then we carried _____ the stones in front of it.
6. I have _____ lived and worked in Barbados.
7. The door was covered _____ plants and a small tree.
8. The family tells us the _____ place.
9. These were questions _____ answers.
10. All nine of us pushed _____.

D. Make sentences with these words. Keep the words in the same order.

1. I, choose, job
2. man, afraid, crypt
3. give, key, family
4. grandfather, put, crypt
5. crypt, own, family
6. family, move, coffin
7. man, carry, knife
8. I, push, door
9. feel, stone, wall
10. police, watch, crypt

E. Write T (for True) if you think that the sentence is true. Write F (for False) if you think that it is not true.

1. The writer did not choose his job.
2. A crypt is a house of stones for the coffins of dead people.
3. There are not many crypts in Barbados now.
4. The writer's men will open an old crypt, but they will not build a new one.
5. Body Three's family is angry with the writer.
6. There were three other bodies in Body Three's first crypt.
7. The writer opened Body Three's first crypt with a key.
8. A cloud covered the sun when the writer walked into the crypt.
9. There was only one coffin in the crypt.
10. The men were afraid to open the second crypt, but they needed the money.

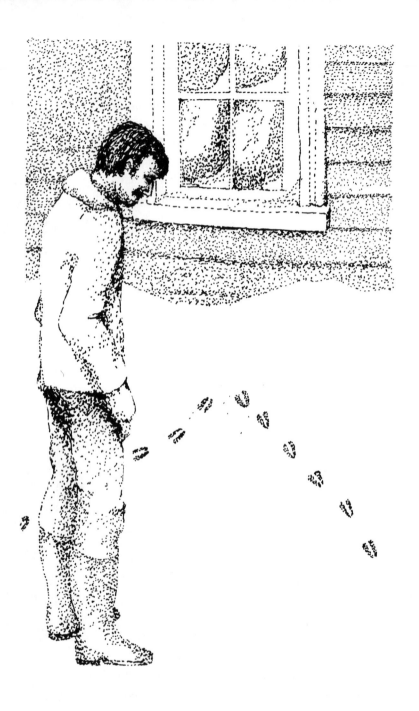

# 6

## Who Looked in the Window Last Night?

Devonshire, England, is beautiful country, with fruit trees, farms, cows, horses, and very blue skies. People work hard from early morning to night, but the earth gives them plenty of food. Most of the people are honest and kind, and they love their families. They like their neighbors, too. If these things are true, why did the **Devil** visit Devonshire in February of 1855?

On the afternoon of February 7, clouds covered the sun over Devonshire. People looked up at the dark sky and said, "It will snow tonight." William Davies, the **baker** in a small town, agreed about the weather. He needed milk for later in the week, but he decided to go at once to the farm. He did not want to make the trip in the snow. His horse was old, and the trip always seemed longer in the snow. When Davies arrived home again with the milk, he left his **wagon** outside his store. When he saw his wagon the next day, he was afraid.

Also on the afternoon of February 7, Grace Marlowe washed

all the windows of her house. When she saw the clouds, she was angry for a minute. It *always* snowed or rained after she cleaned her windows. Then she smiled. Her two children loved the snow. They liked to play in it. But the next day the two boys were afraid to go out into their own yard.

After it snowed, other people acted the same as William Davies and the Marlowe boys. Men did not go to their jobs. Chickens and cows got no food. Women did no shopping. Children did not carry in wood for fires. People just stayed in their houses and looked at the snow. They were afraid of the small **footprints** in the snow. Were they really the Devil's footprints?

A baker cannot sleep late in the morning. Usually he is the first person awake in a town. On February 8, William Davies was washed, dressed, and ready for work by four o'clock. It was still dark outside, but the moon was shining. Davies saw snow on the ground in front of his house. "I am glad I got the milk yesterday," he thought.

Davies made his bread in a small store next to his home. It was just across his front yard. When he went out the door of his house, he stopped in surprise. He usually made the first footprints in new snow. But this time there was already a **line** of footprints in the snow. They went up to his window, then away across the yard.

Davies followed the strange footprints. They were bigger than any bird's foot. And they made only one line in the snow, one footprint in front of another. A person made *two* lines. These footprints were like the shoe of a small horse—if a horse jumped on one leg. Whose footprints were they? Davies did not know.

The footprints seemed to stop next to Davies' wagon, which was full of snow. But when Davies looked up at the top of the wagon, he saw footprints up there, too. Where did the visitor climb up? The snow was not touched at any other place on the wagon. There was just the line of footprints on the ground, and then more footprints on top of the wagon. Davies felt a little afraid because he did not understand this. But his work was waiting. He went into his store, and began to make bread.

Soon the sun was climbing in the sky, and the people of the town were dressing or eating breakfast. When the people looked out their windows, they all saw the same thing: footprints below the window! The footprints went from one window to another, from one house to another. Every family in town found them. And, like William Davies, they did not know whose footprints they were.

At first, people thought that the footprints were interesting. But then news arrived from other towns in Devonshire. The footprints, still in a line, were in every place, at every house and window, for more than 100 miles. How was this done? And who did it? This news seemed dangerous.

People became more afraid when they heard later news. In many places, the line of footprints stopped in front of a high wall and began again on top of the wall. It was like the footprints on William Davies' wagon. In other places the footprints stopped at a river and started again in the snow across the river. Now people began to speak of the Devil, and they went back to their homes. Inside their homes they held their children close.

All over England, newspapers wrote the story of the Devil's visit to Devonshire. William Davies, Grace Marlowe, and their neighbors were famous. Some people's photographs were used by the newspapers. The people of Devonshire lived as before: Davies made bread every day; Grace watched her boys. But when it snowed, they remembered the strange visitor. They locked their doors and sat near the fire. And every person had the same thought: "Will the Devil look in my window again tonight?"

The Devil did not visit Devonshire again. But perhaps he will, the next time it snows.

**New Words**

**a baker**    Someone who makes bread and cakes.

*a baker*

**the Devil**    Satan, Lucifer, Beelzebub, Iblis, Mephistopheles. The very bad one.

*the Devil*

*footprints*

**a footprint**    What we sometimes see where someone or some animal has walked.

**a line**    Things one after the other.

*a line*

*line of footprints*

**a wagon**    Something which is used to carry things in; it does not have an engine, and it is pulled.

*a wagon*

**EXERCISES**

A. Choose the right answer.

1. The people in Devonshire

   a. like the snow.
   b. are honest and kind, and they love their families.
   c. stay in their houses and look at the snow.

2. The people knew it was going to snow because

   a. the sky was dark.
   b. the baker needed milk.
   c. Grace Marlowe washed her windows.

3. William Davies did not want to go to the farm in the snow because

   a. he was afraid of the Devil.
   b. his horse was old, and the trip always seemed longer in the snow.
   c. he agreed about the weather.

4. On the afternoon of February 7, Grace Marlowe

   a. was angry with her two boys.
   b. played in the snow.
   c. washed all the windows of her house.

5. Who is usually the first person awake in a town?

   a. The teacher.
   b. The policeman.
   c. The baker.

6. What did William Davies see when he went out the door of his house?

   a. Grace Marlowe.
   b. A line of footprints.
   c. His old horse.

7. At first, people thought that the footprints were

   a. interesting.
   b. stupid.
   c. lucky.

8. The line of footprints was

   a. more than 100 miles long.
   b. almost 100 miles long.

    c. more than 125 miles long.

9. People thought that the footprints were made by

    a. Grace Marlowe's boys.
    b. the Devil.
    c. a bird.

10. When it snowed, the people of Devonshire

    a. made bread.
    b. locked their doors.
    c. made footprints in the snow.

B. Choose the answer which explains the word or words that look different.

1. They like their *neighbors.*

    a. Their families.
    b. The people who live near them.
    c. Their children.

2. In the afternoon, *clouds covered the sun.*

    a. It was cloudy and the sky was dark.
    b. The sun was shining.
    c. It was raining.

3. *A baker cannot sleep late in the morning.*

    a. A baker can stay in bed in the morning.
    b. A baker need not get up early in the morning.
    c. A baker must get up early in the morning.

4. "*I am glad* I got the milk yesterday."

    a. He is happy.
    b. He is sorry.
    c. He is angry.

5. Davies followed the *strange* footprints.

    a. Large.
    b. Not usual.
    c. Quiet.

C. Put the right word in every sentence.

early, ready, next, usually, already, another, than, whose, full, before

1. He was _____ for work by four o'clock.

2. They made one line in the snow, one footprint in front of _____ .
3. He _____ made the first footprints in new snow.
4. _____ footprints were they?
5. The people of Devonshire lived as _____ .
6. People work hard from _____ morning to night.
7. Davies made his bread in a small store_____ to his house.
8. But this time there was _____ a line of footprints in the snow.
9. The wagon was _____ of snow.
10. The footprints were bigger _____ any bird's foot.

D. Make sentences with these words. Keep the words in the same order.

1. people, look, sky
2. leave, wagon, store
3. child, love, snow
4. chicken, get, food
5. make, bread, store
6. like, shoe, horse
7. print, big, bird
8. where, visitor, climb
9. begin, make, bread
10. newspaper, write, story

E. Write T (for True) if you think that the sentence is true. Write F (for False) if you think that it is not true.

1. People work hard in Devonshire.
2. William Davies was a baker.
3. Grace Marlowe had two children.
4. William Davies woke up at four o'clock.
5. On February 8, Davies made the first footprints in the snow.
6. The prints were like the shoe of a horse.
7. The prints were smaller than a bird's foot.
8. Davies' wagon was full of milk that morning.
9. There were footprints on top of the wagon.
10. The line of footprints was about 100 miles long.

## A Visit to an Eskimo Village

A.  1b, 2a, 3c, 4b, 5b, 6a, 7c, 8b, 9a, 10c

B.  1c, 2a, 3b, 4a, 5c

C.  1 either, 2 still, 3 like, 4 beside, 5 alive, 6 over, 7 afraid, 8 with, 9 outside, 10 empty

E.  1T, 2F, 3F, 4T, 5T, 6F, 7T, 8T, 9F, 10F


## The Luck of James Bartley

A.  1b, 2a, 3b, 4b, 5c, 6c, 7c, 8a, 9c, 10a

B.  1c, 2a, 3c, 4a, 5c

C.  1 against, 2 away, 3 forward, 4 to, 5 last, 6 again, 7 at, 8 inside, 9 like, 10 between

E.  1T, 2F, 3T, 4T, 5T, 6F, 7T, 8F, 9F, 10F

**The Man who Dreamed the News**

A.    1b, 2c, 3b, 4c, 5a, 6b, 7b, 8a, 9c, 10a

B.    1c, 2b, 3a, 4a, 5b

C.    1 into, 2 back, 3 as, 4 many, 5 about, 6 who, 7 near, 8 through, 9 than, 10 for

E.    1T, 2T, 3F, 4F, 5T, 6F, 7F, 8F, 9T, 10T


**A Fine Afternoon in December**

A.    1b, 2b, 3c, 4a, 5a, 6c, 7a, 8b, 9a, 10c

B.    1a, 2c, 3a, 4b, 5c

C.    1 into, 2 over, 3 either, 4 everywhere, 5 because, 6 off, 7 already, 8 plenty, 9 just, 10 second

E.    1T, 2F, 3F, 4T, 5T, 6T, 7F, 8T, 9F, 10T


**The Coffins of Barbados**

A.    1c, 2a, 3b, 4a, 5c, 6b, 7c, 8a, 9c, 10a

B.    1c, 2a, 3b, 4b, 5a

C.    1 yet, 2 enough, 3 against, 4 ready, 5 away, 6 always, 7 by, 8 right, 9 without, 10 together

E.    1T, 2T, 3F, 4F, 5T, 6F, 7F, 8T, 9F, 10T


**Who Looked in the Window Last Night?**

A.    1b, 2a, 3b, 4c, 5c, 6b, 7a, 8a, 9b, 10b

B.    1b, 2a, 3c, 4a, 5b

C.    1 ready, 2 another, 3 usually, 4 whose, 5 before, 6 early, 7 next 8 already, 9 full, 10 than

E.    1T, 2T, 3T, 4F, 5F, 6T, 7F, 8F, 9T, 10T